A Month of Creative Writing Prompts

Written by
Cindy Barden

Editors: Barbara G. Hoffman and Michael Batty

Cover and Interior Design: Good Neighbor Press, Inc.

Illustrator: Chris Nye

FS112130 September Journal Jumpstarts


23740 Hawthorne Boulevard
Torrance, CA 90505-5927

# Table of Contents

## September

# Introduction

**An empty journal is filled with infinite possibilities.**

Writing regularly in a journal helps us to develop our imaginations, encourages us to express our thoughts, feelings, and dreams, and provides a way to communicate experiences in words and pictures. Many students feel frustrated when asked to keep a journal. They may not be sure of what to write, or they may be intimidated by a blank sheet of paper. Even professional writers occasionally face "writer's block." The Journal Jumpstarts series provides ideas and suggestions for daily journal entries. Each book contains 29 jumpstarts. You could give each student a photocopy of the same page or provide a variety of pages and allow students to choose their own topics. You may have students who will be able to sit and write without jumpstarts. At times students may prefer to express their thoughts through drawings or with a combination of drawings and writing. Be encouraging!

Through making regular entries in journals, students become more observant of themselves and the world around them. Journal writing on a regular basis strengthens students' attention spans and abilities to focus. Keeping journals promotes self-esteem because students are doing something for themselves—not for grades or in competition with others. A journal can become an essential friend, a confidante in times of personal crisis.

Encourage students to get into the journal habit by setting aside writing time every day at about the same time, such as first thing in the morning or shortly before lunch. Share their journal time by writing in your own journal. What better way to encourage a good habit than by example!

Note: Assure students that what they write is confidential. Provide a safe, secure place for students to store their journals. Respect their privacy, as you would expect your privacy to be respected—read their journals by invitation only.

Name ______________________ Date ______________

# Personal Best

The ten best things about me are . . .

Name ______________________ Date ______________

# Goals

My three most important goals for this school year are . . .

Name ______________________ Date ______________

# My Schedule

You may have a busy schedule—a list of things that you do at the same time every day or week. Maybe you take out the trash on Tuesday nights or practice baseball on Saturday mornings. You probably go to school every weekday morning. Describe your schedule. Is there anything you'd like to change about it? Why or why not?

Name ______________________ Date ______________

# Responsibilities

You may have been put in charge of certain things at home or school, like washing dishes, feeding a pet, or keeping your desk tidy. These are responsibilities. What are your responsibilities? How do you feel about them?

Name ______________________ Date ______________

# Wish upon a Star

"Starlight, star bright, first star I see tonight,
I wish I may, I wish I might,
Have the wish I wish tonight."

What do you wish for when you see the first star? Write about why your wish is important to you.

Name ______________________________ Date ____________________

# A Relative

Write about a member of your family and explain why that person is unique and special to you.

Name ______________________ Date ______________

# Family Fun

Write about something that you and your family enjoy doing together.

Name ______________________ Date ______________

# Favorite Toy

Do you have a favorite toy? Describe it and tell why you like it the best.

Name ______________________ Date ______________

# Someone Special

Who would you most like to meet? Explain why you would like to meet him or her.

Name ______________________ Date ____________

# My Teacher Appreciates Me

Write a nice thing that your teacher this year or your teacher last year said to you. Write about how that made you feel.

Name ______________________ Date ______________

# Making New Friends

Being in school is a great opportunity to make new friends. Write about a new friend that you've made this school year. Explain why you like this person. What kinds of things could you do together?

Name ______________________ Date ______________

# Bzzzzzzzzzzzzzzz

If you could be a kind of insect, which kind would you like to be? Describe what you think it would be like to be that kind of insect.

Name ______________________________ Date ______________

# Treetop View

Imagine you are a tree. You're tall and majestic. You've been watching what goes on around you for a long, long time. Write observations and thoughts from your point of view as a tree.

Name ______________________ Date ______________

# Anthem

Write a song or poem that could be used as an anthem for your school or your community.

Name ______________________ Date ____________

# Tomorrow

Write about three things that would make you happy if they happened tomorrow.

Name ______________________ Date ______________

# Holiday Inventor

Invent a new holiday for September. Explain when it would take place, what you would call it, why people would like it, and how people would celebrate.

Name ______________________ Date ______________

# In the Future

What do you think you will be like when you go to high school? You will be about thirteen or fourteen years old. Write about how you might look and what might interest you.

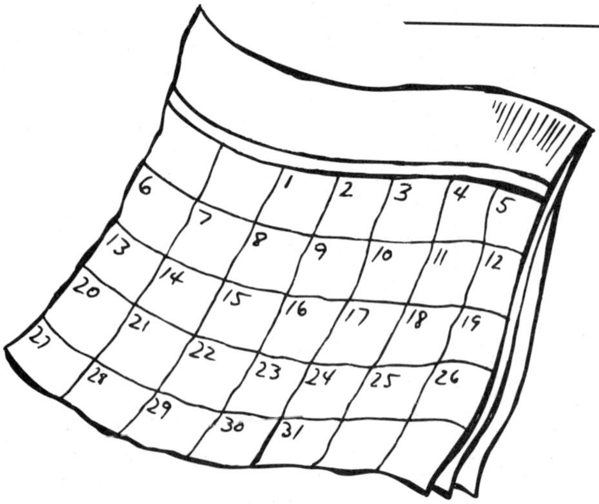

Name ______________________ Date ______________

# Shipwrecked

If you were shipwrecked alone on a deserted island, what are the first three things that you would do?

Name ________________________ Date ____________

# What's for Breakfast?

If you could have anything that you wanted for breakfast, what would you eat? Write about the tastes, textures, and smells of the foods that you enjoy most for breakfast.

MENU

Name ______________________ Date ____________

# Sunday, Sunday

Write about Sundays at school or at home. What do you like most about Sundays? What do you like least?

Name ____________________ Date ____________

# Fall

September is the first month of fall. Describe what makes September days and nights different from summer days and nights. What do you do, see, hear, smell, taste, and feel in September?

Name ______________________ Date ______________

# Funny Money

The money that we use has pictures and writing on it. If you could put new pictures and writing on coins and bills, what would you choose? Describe your new money with words and draw pictures of it on the back of this page or on a separate sheet of paper.

Name ______________________ Date ____________

# Animated Me

Which cartoon character are you most like? Write about how you and that character are similar.

Name ______________________ Date ______________

# School

Write about what you like best and least about your school. If you could change one thing about your school, what would it be? Why?

 

Name ______________________ Date ____________

# Class Rules

Write about a classroom rule that you think is unfair and explain why. What could you do to change it?

Name ______________________ Date ____________

# Six Days a Week

Write about how you would feel if you went to school six days a week instead of five. Would you like it? Why or why not?

Name ______________________ Date ______________

# School Clothes

What should students be allowed to wear to school? Should they be allowed to wear whatever they want, or should they wear uniforms? Explain what you believe with at least two reasons.

Name ______________________ Date ______________

# Writing Sequels

What's the best book that you ever read? Pretend that you are going to write more of the story in another chapter or another book. What would happen in the new part?

Name ______________________ Date ____________

# Secret Staircase

Imagine that you find a secret staircase at your school. Where does it go? Why is it hidden? What happens when you use the stairs?

SCHOOL